Applying for Graduate Admission to US Engineering Schools

Bruce Lindvall, Ph.D.

Copyright © Bruce Lindvall 2024

All Rights Reserved

No part of this publication may be reproduced, distributed, or transmitted in any form or by any means, including photocopying, recording, or other electronic or mechanical methods, without the author's prior written permission, except in the case of brief quotations embodied in critical reviews and certain other non-commercial uses permitted by copyright law. For permission requests, please get in touch with the author.

Contents

Dedication i
Acknowledgments ii
About the Author iii
Author's Note iv
Introduction 1
Why Graduate School? 4
How early do you start planning? 6
Gaining Research Experience 8
Decentralized Admissions 10
M.S. vs. Ph.D. Study 12
Test Scores (GRE and English Proficiency Tests) 14
Essay Questions 17
Letters of Recommendation 19
Rankings and ASEE Profiles 22
Diversity in Graduate Programs 24
Tracking Your Applications 26
The Council of Graduate Schools and the April 15th Resolution 28
Funding Graduate Study 30
Applying for Outside Funding 32
Who Can Assist You? 34
Getting the Word Out about Graduate Engineering Opportunities 36
Final Thoughts 38
Resources 40

Dedication

It is truly impossible to name all the university colleagues, students, and friends who have supported me and encouraged me to write this book. I especially want to thank my sons, Heath and Troy, for their enduring love and support in my career in higher education.

Acknowledgments

Three universities, Purdue University, the University of Kansas, and Northwestern University, provided me with opportunities to work with students in recruitment, admissions, and student affairs roles in my five decades in higher education. I am indebted to them for those opportunities.

About the Author

Bruce Lindvall spent 51 years in higher education, with his most recent 18 years in graduate engineering admissions at Northwestern University. He is passionate about helping students navigate the graduate engineering admissions process.

He has a B.S. degree in mathematics, an M.S. in counseling, and a Ph.D. in higher education administration, all from Purdue University in West Lafayette, Indiana.

Author's Note

Dear reader,

After a 51-year career in higher education, I have retired and written this book that will help prospective graduate students who are in the process of applying for admission. I will outline several aspects of the book.

What is outlined in the book will help students around the world prepare and apply for M.S. and Ph.D. admission in graduate engineering. I have been speaking nationally about graduate study in engineering for the last 15-plus years. In the United States there are far too many undergraduate engineering students who immediately join the workforce with high-paying salaries. Over 70% of the engineering Ph.D. students and over 85% of the engineering M.S. students are from other countries. This book will also help international students submit stronger applications as they apply for graduate engineering study in the United States. There are certainly many audiences beyond undergraduate engineering students who want to apply for graduate study in engineering. That will be shared later.

My background includes an M.S. in mathematics, an M.S. in Counseling, and a Ph.D. in higher education administration (all from Purdue University). My 51 years in higher education were spent at Purdue (undergraduate, pharmacy, and veterinary school admissions), the University of Kansas (undergraduate and graduate admissions), and Northwestern University (engineering graduate admissions). In addition to this background, for the last 18 years I spent working with high school and undergraduate students who were interested in pursuing graduate study in engineering. With my background in higher education for over half a century, I never encountered anyone else who ever had a broader and more in-depth background in college admissions in the United States. I humbly submit this background to illustrate that I have excellent experiences to author a book of this magnitude.

The content of the book has many potential audiences:

- High school students and parents around the world
- High school counselors in the United States
- Undergraduate engineering students in the United States
- Undergraduate engineering students around the world, especially from China and India
- University counselors and faculty in engineering schools both in the United States and around the world who encourage students to pursue graduate study and help them apply for graduate admission
- Major companies and national labs whose employees can encourage undergraduate interns to pursue graduate study instead of immediately joining the workforce in the United States

What motivated me to do this when I retired at the age of 75? Unlike so many engineering students, my goal was not to see how much money I can make. I have had a lifetime career of encouraging and helping high school and college students attain more education so they can have a more productive and fulfilling career. You could say that it has been my life's calling.

What are the problems as I see it?

- Ph.D. study in engineering is fully funded, yet at least 70% of the Ph.D. graduates are from other countries and many companies and national labs cannot hire them because of national security issues. Universities and governmental agencies in the United States provide a fully funded Ph.D., yet we are sending international students back to their home countries to help the economies and defense programs in those countries. Few in the United States seem to grasp this.

- My primary audience is students so we can encourage them to complete graduate study in engineering before they embark on their engineering careers. Money does not buy happiness. It is having a fulfilling career that excites you about getting up each day and going to work. I know. I experienced that for 51 years!

- As anyone reads through the book, they will learn things they never knew. This book has some incredible insights for all audiences so we can help educate them on what is involved and what are the rewards.

- While many universities have offices that prepare students to go to medical school or law school, very few have an office or a person who helps engineering students apply to graduate school. As hard as I tried at Northwestern's McCormick School of Engineering, I was one of the few who kept doing this. Faculty, advisors, and career staff generally focused on two things: helping students graduate with a bachelor's degree and enter the workforce. That is true essentially at all engineering schools in the United States. After national presentations and working through e-mails, prospective graduate engineering students shared the same experiences from their undergraduate universities. There is a national need and worldwide audience for this.

Thank you for taking time to read this.

Most sincerely,

Bruce A. Lindvall

Introduction

For most prospective engineering graduate students this will be the first time applying for graduate admission. Sadly, there is little in place to help students navigate what can be a confusing, frustrating, and stressful situation. This is something the author personally experienced as he helped students apply for both undergraduate and graduate admissions.

As a starting point, these general points are made to set the stage for engineering graduate admissions. They are shared in no order and will be expanded upon further in the chapters of this book.

- Graduate admission is a decentralized process, with most decisions made within the academic program or academic department.

- Most Ph.D. programs allow a student to apply with only an undergraduate degree. In most cases, an M.S. degree is not required for Ph.D. admission.

- Nearly all engineering Ph.D. programs are fully funded with paid tuition and an annual stipend to cover living expenses. Many Ph.D. programs will partially or fully cover health insurance. While some M.S. programs are funded or even partially funded, many are not.

- Most M.S. and Ph.D. programs have more international students than US students and permanent residents of the US.

- Since COVID in 2020, with the closing of test centers, many graduate engineering programs no longer require the GRE. Very few require the GRE. Some have a GRE optional policy. Another group of engineering schools do not use the GRE at all.

- International applicants must demonstrate English proficiency. That can be done in several ways and includes a degree from a university where English is the language of instruction or minimum scores on the TOEFL, IELTS, Duolingo, or Michigan English Test.

- Graduate admission involves the holistic review of applications. That means that many factors are taken into consideration, including the overall academic record, grade point average, trends in grades, test scores, letters of recommendation, research experience, leadership roles, interviews (in-person, phone, and Zoom), overcoming adversity in life, etc. The overall grade point may be the best predictor of academic success at the graduate level, but many factors are used in the overall review of an application.

- Rankings can play a role in determining the quality of a graduate program, but another source will be introduced that will provide important data about each graduate program.

- With the US Supreme Court decision in June 2023, the landscape has shifted with the addition of many new essay questions as part of the admissions process.

- Most graduate programs require an application fee, and in some cases students (US and international) may qualify for an application fee waiver.

This book is written to help all prospective graduate engineering students apply for graduate admission. For US students, it serves to help more US students apply for and attend graduate school in engineering. For international students, it serves to help them understand the process better and to help them submit strong graduate school applications.

This section serves to help motivate students to carefully read through the chapters of this book and prepare strong graduate school applications.

Why Graduate School?

This is an important question that each prospective graduate student needs to answer. While engineering students with a bachelor's degree are likely to be hired into entry-level positions with excellent starting salaries, graduate school (1-5 or more years) is an investment into a future career in engineering. Of course, a graduate degree will result in higher-level positions and higher salaries, but students need to understand that a career is so much more than how much money can be earned with a bachelor's degree in engineering.

It should also be noted that most Ph.D. graduates do not end up in tenure-track positions in academia. Being a faculty member in an engineering school is an option, but most Ph.D. engineering graduates work in private industry, national labs, or start-up companies.

A graduate degree in engineering allows entry into higher-level positions that can be very rewarding, more challenging, and lead to greater achievements and fulfillment in a career.

Many universities have career planning and placement offices. That, in turn, may allow students to set up internships. When students work in those settings or even have summer research experiences at a university, they should look around and see what roles individuals have and find out about each person's educational background that prepared them for their work.

Going to graduate school is not something to do if you cannot find a job. Graduate school is an investment in your future that will pay great dividends over a lifetime career. It is what can motivate an individual to be excited to get up each day and head to work to make greater contributions to your employer and the world beyond!

How early do you start planning?

When students approach their high school years, usually students and parents have a meeting with a school counselor to plan four years of high school education. Planning for graduate school does not need to be any different. On the other hand, the junior year of undergraduate study and the summer before the senior year of undergraduate study can be critical times to finalize plans to prepare for graduate school study and applications.

Certainly, some of the very best graduate school applicants knew when enrolling in undergraduate study that they wanted to go to graduate school in engineering. That usually means they had excellent grades, followed a strong curriculum, sought out academic year research opportunities and summer research opportunities, looked for leadership roles in student organizations, and other related experiences to prepare for graduate admissions and graduate study.

For those who decide later, then the junior year and the summer before the senior year can be critical to identifying potential graduate schools, seeking their final summer research experience, lining up recommendations, preparing potential essays, taking appropriate tests, and other factors to begin the application process.

Some prospective students will wait until the fall of their senior year to begin doing all of this. On one hand, seniors are trying to finish up an undergraduate degree and prepare for graduate admissions, and that can be a difficult mix which leads to a very stressful fall term.

It is never too early to plan for graduate study. The earlier this is done, the better off an applicant will be in the graduate admissions process.

Gaining Research Experience

While many M.S. programs do not involve research or a thesis as course-based M.S. programs, all Ph.D. study involves in-depth research. If an applicant is undecided about M.S. vs. Ph.D. study, then research experience as an undergraduate student can help a student decide if research is something they enjoy and would want to pursue in an M.S. with a thesis or a Ph.D. program. For those students who know that Ph.D. study is in their future, gaining research experience is critical.

Many US universities have undergraduate research available for engineering students. It is important to seek out those opportunities as early as the freshman year. There may be sources at the university or within the engineering school to pay the student for their research. Even as a high school student or a new university freshman, it is recommended that students seek out those opportunities and gain research experience as early as possible.

Going beyond what is available on the college campus during undergraduate study, there are many summer opportunities that come with excellent funding. It is important to note that many of these opportunities are available to only US citizens and permanent residents.

The best source of summer research experiences is with the National Science Foundation (NSF) through their Research Experiences for Undergraduates (REU) programs. This NSF website lists programs that can be sorted by academic area or by state:

https://www.nsf.gov/crssprgm/reu/reu_search.jsp

Within the Big Ten Conference, there is the Summer Research Opportunity Program (SROP):

https://apps.btaa.org/srop/apply

A Google search for SURF (Summer Undergraduate Research Fellowship) programs will also yield a significant number of summer research programs in US universities.

It should be noted that most programs provide a significant stipend, paid room and board, and perhaps paid transportation to and from the student residence.

International students studying in the US are typically not eligible for these programs.

Application deadlines are usually in January and February each year, so students are encouraged to apply early and to apply for multiple programs. Applying for these summer research programs is also excellent preparation for the graduate admission process.

These are excellent programs with research opportunities, and many US students are not aware of them.

Decentralized Admissions

Unlike undergraduate admissions in the US, graduate admission is very decentralized.

Here are some very important factors to remember:

- Graduate admissions from one university to another can be very different.
- Graduate admissions across one university can vary greatly.
- Graduate admissions within an academic college/school can be quite different.
- Universities with excellent websites should have an admissions section for each academic program/department. Within that website there may be separate sections for M.S. and Ph.D. admissions.

So, how does an applicant handle this? First and foremost, never assume that anything is the same across universities or even within a university or within an academic school/college.

An applicant needs to drill down into the specific websites for the program/department to which you are applying. Websites should contain application deadlines, the application process, required materials, required tests, listing of faculty members, and the research being done within the department and by individual faculty members.

One key point of advice is for each prospective applicant to thoroughly read a website *before* writing to the program with your questions. That is why these websites exist to answer basic questions so the applicant can learn a great deal about a specific academic department or program. Never write to a university, asking questions that are readily answered on a website.

In another chapter, tracking your applications and key contacts will be addressed.

M.S. vs. Ph.D. Study

One question that often arises is whether a student wants to complete an M.S. or Ph.D.. Here are some basic points to keep in mind.

- Is your goal to complete a Ph.D.? If so, you should apply for admission if the program allows direct admission from an undergraduate program into Ph.D. study.

- Most engineering Ph.D. graduates do not go into academia. Do not assume that a Ph.D. is only for those individuals who want to go into academia. Many major companies in the US and many national labs hire Ph.D. graduates.

- Many M.S. programs are not fully funded, while Ph.D. studies should be fully funded. There is no need to accumulate debt with an M.S. study when you can be funded with Ph.D. study.

Some universities will allow students to apply for Ph.D. admission and then be considered for M.S. admission if not admitted to Ph.D. study. It is important to check this possibility as applications are being submitted. Sometimes students have records that will not qualify for Ph.D. admission at top universities. Lower grade point averages and/or the lack of research experience may eliminate an applicant from Ph.D. admissions. One way to overcome not being admitted to Ph.D. study is to apply for M.S. admission, undertake research through an M.S. with a thesis, strengthen the academic record and research experience, find a faculty member who becomes your advocate, and then apply for Ph.D. admission after that. Applying for Ph.D. admission with a fallback opportunity for M.S. admission can be a strong plan to follow. One never knows if the grades and research background will be sufficient for Ph.D. admission to a particular program.

It is important to solicit advice about universities where you should apply for admission. Like what many high school students do, you can apply for some top programs and then have others where admission is not as competitive.

Whether you are entering undergraduate education or graduate study, your success is more about what you do with the educational opportunity than where you were admitted for undergraduate or graduate study.

Seek advice from faculty at your university, others from internships and research experiences, and individuals in career planning offices who can help you plan your course of seeking M.S. or Ph.D. study.

Test Scores (GRE and English Proficiency Tests)

First, let's address the issue of the GRE. During the pandemic in 2020, many test centers around the world were closed. That meant that engineering graduate programs could not require or secure GRE scores from all their applicants. Since then, these three policies have emerged.

- Some programs/departments are now requiring the GRE since test centers have reopened.
- Many programs/departments are allowing the GRE to be optional.
- Some programs do not require or use the GRE at all.

The GRE can be an expensive test for many and typically involves time for prospective students to prepare for the exam. Here are some considerations:

- Some applicants have strong overall records and will be admitted without GRE scores. A lower score on the GRE could jeopardize admissions.
- Other applicants have average to perhaps below-average overall records and very strong GRE scores. Those applicants may be boosted into admission consideration with those scores.

- Some applicants will come from lesser-known universities both in the US and in other countries, and admission committees may struggle with an academic record from that institution. Strong GRE scores may enhance that applicant into a more favorable position to be admitted.

The issue of whether to take the GRE is a very difficult question, and it may be important to contact an individual program/department to seek their input and even ask how many applicants submitted GRE scores.

Secondly, let's address English proficiency. Most application pools are dominated by international applicants, and English proficiency is critical to engineering graduate study in the US. Here are the ways that US universities determine the English proficiency of an applicant.

- Completion of a degree (undergraduate or master's degree) where English is the language of instruction.
- Country of citizenship where English is the primary language of that country
- Minimum score on the TOEFL
- Minimum score on the IELTS
- Minimum score on the Duolingo
- Minimum score on the MET (Michigan English Test)

It is extremely important to check the departmental/program website to determine what is required. This can vary considerably from one university to the other. Likewise, some of the English proficiency tests are not available around the world.

Essay Questions

For many years, graduate admission in engineering has involved one or more essay questions as part of the application process. This perhaps has the most variance of all the required materials in the graduate engineering admission process.

The primary question has typically been what is referenced as the "personal statement" or "statement of purpose." It is very important that you carefully read individual websites to determine what is needed. Never assume that what you have written for one university can be used for the next application. This question may focus more on your past. Others focus more on your future research interests and the faculty research that is of interest to you. There is a big difference between these two alternatives. Some universities will break this up into more than one question.

Some universities will have a separate question (not required) that allows an applicant to share something they may not have learned about you from the standard application. This allows an applicant to share what may have caused grades to drop or even increase over time. An applicant may have encountered a personal issue or illness that created a drop in grades. Some applicants may have encountered the divorce of parents, the illness and even the death of a loved one. Use this opportunity to explain any of these, but do not use it as an excuse or to blame someone else or circumstances for an irregularity in an academic record.

This optional question will also allow you to share more about personal projects you have undertaken on your own, such as research, extra-curricular activities, leadership, applying for grants or fellowships, being a teaching assistant, studying abroad, and anything else that is not part of the questions on the application or perhaps limited by what you can share in a resume or CV.

Most recently the decision by the Supreme Court of the US in June 2023 has caused many universities to make changes in the application and add a new essay question. For many universities, diversity in the graduate study body is very important. The Supreme Court decision ruled that race cannot be used in admission. Some universities eliminated a question about race as part of the application. Other universities are collecting the information but are not sharing it with the faculty and staff who are reviewing the applications.

This is new in 2024 admissions. In place of that collection of information about race, there is a range of questions that are being used by universities. The questions can involve learning more about the applicant's background, what the applicant has overcome in life, what the applicant can add to the diversity of the graduate student body, etc. This is so new that it is difficult to share more currently.

It is important to read the application instructions of what is expected in response to this new essay question as well as the other essay questions. The responses to these questions are critical in the holistic review of an application.

Letters of Recommendation

Most engineering graduate school applications require multiple letters of recommendation.

The first question is whom to ask. It is important to make a list of potential recommenders and then contact them. If possible, it is recommended that the request be made in person. Why? By asking someone in person, their reaction, time responding, and excitement (or lack thereof) is in plain view during the in-person request. Asking people within academia is best, especially for them to comment on the academic ability, research experience, and/or leadership of an applicant. There are some applications that will give guidance on whom to ask and even whom not to ask, such as coaches, pastors, etc. Once again, it is critically important to read the recommendation instructions for each program. Do not assume that you will use the same people for all your applications. It is also suggested that each recommender be given an idea of how many requests each recommender will receive.

Most applications will request three recommendations. However, it is important to read application instructions for each department or program. Sometimes, programs will say that three are recommended while two are required. How does an applicant decide? First, three recommendations is not necessarily the best answer. If there is a drop-off with the third recommendation, do not use the third if only two are required. Nearly all recommendations are quite strong. One mediocre or weaker recommendation can easily remove an applicant from further consideration. Do not ask to submit more recommendations than are recommended or required. It is always important to follow application instructions.

If an applicant has done considerable research, then the faculty member in charge of that research group is critical. Not having a recommendation from that research experience can raise serious concerns for the faculty reviewer. If the applicant has worked primarily with a graduate student or postdoc, it may be possible for that person to draft a letter that is signed by the faculty member in charge.

Whether an individual is a full professor, associate professor, or assistant professor is usually not that important. What is most important is how well the recommender knows the applicant and what they convey in the letter about academic, research, and leadership backgrounds.

Once the group of recommenders is identified, a resume or CV should be shared with them well in advance of the deadline for submitting the recommendation.

Most applications involve online systems. That typically means two important points. First, submitted and missing materials can be tracked by the applicant. Second, most systems provide the applicant an opportunity to have reminders sent for missing recommendations. It is the responsibility of the applicant to track the completeness of submitted applications.

One final point needs to be made. Most programs have a strict deadline for submitting an application. What may be confusing is when the application must be completed with all required materials. Once again, it is important for each applicant to track deadlines and the completion of each application. Many universities will give extra time to have recommendations submitted. Keep in mind, however, that many applications are not reviewed until the application file is complete.

Rankings and ASEE Profiles

Prospective students often ask how many applications should be submitted in an admissions cycle and to what universities applications should be submitted. Those are excellent questions with no easy answers.

One starting point would be looking at the rankings of graduate engineering programs and not just the overall ranking of a university. In the US, the most popular rankings are available through US News and World Reports. There are overall rankings for academic schools or colleges, as well as rankings by specific departments. International rankings include QS World University Rankings and Times Higher Education.

Within the rankings and with an understanding of where applicants may fit into qualifying for admission, a prospective applicant can begin reviewing a set of universities where applications can be submitted. Many students apply to approximately 8-10, or even more, graduate programs.

One method to use is to rank the preference of schools and begin applying to those at the top of the list. The time to prepare applications, the time to research each program, and the cost of application fees may cause a student to stop submitting applications. For example, a student may have a list of 20 possible schools and begin submitting applications at the top of the list. After considerable time spent and after paying application fees, the student may stop with the tenth application.

An unknown source to many prospective students is the American Society for Engineering Education (ASEE). Within their website, they offer profiles of graduates, enrolled students, faculty, and research expenditures at each M.S. and Ph.D. engineering program in the United States. The profiles of enrolled students are rather granular, so students can see how many students are enrolled in each program, including gender, race, citizenship, full-time vs. part-time, etc. These data points can be especially important for prospective students to learn about the size of the program and the composition of the graduate student body. The breakdown includes each university's individual engineering graduate programs at both the M.S. and Ph.D. levels. The profiles also include undergraduate enrollments:

https://americansocietyforengineeringeducation.shinyapps.io/profiles/

These data are especially important as the prospective student considers how they fit into a particular graduate program. Objective data found in the ASEE Profiles can be important in determining where to submit applications and in making a final decision on where to enroll.

Diversity in Graduate Programs

In the United States, there has been great debate over the diversity of graduate student populations. That means that many graduate engineering programs have strived to have more women and more underrepresented minority students in their graduate programs. As indicated in the prior chapter, the American Society for Engineering Education (ASEE) profiles graduate student enrollments (gender, race, citizenship, and full-time or part-time status). In a similar manner, the profiles of faculty within each department are shared. For a prospective student seeking diversity in the graduate study body and/or the faculty, this is an invaluable resource. The link to the ASEE website is shared again:

https://americansocietyforengineeringeducation.shinyapps.io/profiles/

It is the opinion of many educators that a diverse graduate student body is invaluable in preparing graduate students to face their future careers in an ever-changing, diverse workforce.

Many prospective students seek diversity in their potential graduate student programs and universities, and there is no better source than the ASEE Profiles.

With the decision of the US Supreme Court in June 2023, the Supreme Court ruled that race cannot be used in admissions. The higher education landscape is in a period of uncertainty, so the ASEE Profiles will become even more important. On an annual basis engineering schools submit responses to a lengthy ASEE survey to provide the data on student enrollments, graduates, faculty, and research expenditures. The data set for each fall is submitted at the end of the fall term, and the new data typically appear later in the spring from the prior fall.

Within the United States since 1971, the GEM National Consortium has worked with universities, companies, and national labs to educate a more diverse graduate study body through the GEM Fellowship Program:

https://www.gemfellowship.org/gem-fellowship-program/

This is one of the few fellowship programs that serves the full-time M.S. student population. Underrepresented minority students especially should apply for this fellowship program which is open to only US citizens and permanent residents.

As applicants refine their list of potential applications or make a final decision, the data from the ASEE Profiles can be very important.

Tracking Your Applications

With prospective students submitting so many applications, it is recommended that students create a tracking system to better handle multiple applications. Below is a sample of what can be used.

	Univ #1	Univ #2	Univ #3	Univ #4	Univ #5
Program					
Website					
Admission Deadline					
Admission Decision					
Contact					
E-mail					
Phone					
Interview Date					

With many applications in progress, it can be very difficult to keep on top of multiple applications. It is strongly encouraged that each applicant starts the tracking at the beginning. Students often become impatient when hearing from some schools and not others. Perhaps the best advice to be shared is to find a key contact person for each of your applications. That can be a staff member, faculty member, admissions chair, or perhaps someone else. Keep that person's e-mail address and phone number handy.

When questions or concerns arise, reach out to that individual and hopefully have a quick and complete response. If a university is not very responsive, that can be a signal of how the program treats its enrolled students.

The Council of Graduate Schools and the April 15th Resolution

As outlined in prior chapters, the graduate admission process can be quite stressful, and applicants can become quite impatient.

Most US universities belong to the Council of Graduate Schools. The Council of Graduate Schools has an April 15th Resolution that covers the acceptance deadline for funded Ph.D. admission:

https://cgsnet.org/wp-content/uploads/2024/01/CGS_April15_Resolution_Jan22024.pdf

This policy basically states that a Ph.D. applicant should hear from universities by April 15 for fall admissions and that applicants have until April 15 to select a final choice from their several offers of admission.

Keep in mind that some universities move quickly with admission notifications, while others may not notify students until March or even early April. Universities that are listed in this resolution cannot require a decision before April 15th.

This recommendation about Ph.D. admissions can be rather basic. Be patient, and do not be concerned *when* you learn of an admissions decision. After admission and before April 15, many universities pay for students (residing in the United States) to visit campus, meet faculty and students, see facilities, and learn as much as possible while on campus. This can all be very important as an applicant reaches a decision about which offer of admission to accept.

M.S. admissions and deadlines are a very different story. Unless a student is funded, the April 15th deadline does not apply. This can be a much different decision process since many universities require a deposit for M.S. admissions, and the acceptance deadlines can vary significantly. In recent years universities have experienced many M.S. applicants accepting multiple offers of admission. Without a common decision deadline, this can be quite difficult for M.S. applicants, especially when they may be faced with rather significant deposit amounts.

There is nothing wrong with accepting multiple offers or even asking for an extension of a deadline. It is important in the end to communicate final decisions to all universities that have made offers of admission. When admission is accepted, notify others of non-enrollment.

Funding Graduate Study

As mentioned earlier, general statements can be made with great variance across universities.

Let's begin with a Ph.D. study. In the US, the Ph.D. study is generally funded with paid or waived tuition and an annual stipend that should cover living expenses for students in that university setting. It is also possible that the university may partially or fully cover student health insurance. The letter of admission should detail what is being offered with Ph.D. admission. If anything seems to be missing, then communicate with the university and ask for a *response in writing*. This is especially true about health insurance as well as the number of years of funding. Ph.D. funding is typically guaranteed for a minimum of five years.

Annual stipends can vary significantly but should be considered with the cost of living in each university community. Higher stipends are important with a higher cost of living. Student health insurance can cost $5000 or more annually, so it is important to learn if a university is helping pay for student health insurance. All this needs to be clarified before choosing a university for Ph.D. study.

Let's also discuss funding for M.S. students. Some programs do not provide any funding for M.S. study, while others provide partial or perhaps full funding. It is also important to understand the difference in tuition levels at universities in the United States. Public universities have funding from state governments, so the tuition levels are lower than private universities. If a student is considering M.S. study, then there are critical questions to explore. What is the annual cost of tuition and fees? Is any funding available for the M.S. study? If so, under what circumstances? What will the funding cover? Tuition and fees? Is a stipend available? Under what circumstances?

There are several interrelated issues to consider. Is the final goal an M.S. degree or a Ph.D. degree? How much needs to be paid or perhaps borrowed in student loans to complete an M.S. degree?

It may be important to consult family members and key people in higher education to sort through these issues. Sources of advice are outlined in a future chapter.

Applying for Outside Funding

Prospective students who are US citizens are encouraged to apply for the National Science Foundation Graduate Research Fellowship for the first year of Ph.D. study. Having one or more years of funding can make an applicant even more attractive in the admissions process. The deadlines, which vary by subject area, tend to be in October and November each year. The announcement of winners is typically made in March each year, but ahead of the April 15th admission decision deadline.

https://www.nsfgrfp.org/

Unsuccessful undergraduate applicants who are current graduate students (US citizens only) can apply for the NSF Graduate Research Fellowship one time after enrolling in an M.S. or Ph.D. program.

There are other fellowship programs for prospective engineering students who are US citizens or permanent residents. Here are some examples:

Department of Defense NDSEG

https://ndseg.sysplus.com/

SMART Scholarship

https://www.smartscholarship.org/smart/en

Hertz Fellowship

https://www.hertzfoundation.org/the-fellowship/

GEM Fellowship

https://www.gemfellowship.org/gem-fellowship-program/

Certainly, there are other fellowship programs that can be found through Google searches.

These fellowship programs are limited to US citizens and permanent residents. What is the recommendation for international applicants?

Many countries have programs that help fund students from that country to pursue M.S. and Ph.D. studies in the United States. It is recommended that international students learn about these opportunities and apply for them, even if the student is seeking Ph.D. admission in the United States.

It is important to note that most international students in Ph.D. study in the United States are fully funded in the same manner as US citizens and permanent residents. Nevertheless, international students should pursue these opportunities since any Ph.D. applicant with full or even partial funding can be viewed as a more attractive applicant. It is estimated that 70% of the engineering Ph.D. students in the United States are international students. The exact percentages of international Ph.D. populations by university and program are available in the ASEE Profiles.

Who Can Assist You?

Many US engineering schools are focused on helping undergraduate students successfully complete their degrees and secure a well-paying position. Unfortunately, many universities do not have personnel in place to help students apply for admission to graduate engineering programs.

Here are some excellent starting points:

- The family can be involved in working with a student who is contemplating graduate study. It can be important to have their full support, including financial support. Share this book with them!

- If a student has a solid relationship with an undergraduate advisor, the advisor can be an excellent resource for graduate school advice.

- Professors with whom you have taken classes can be excellent resources.

- Some universities offer services in career planning and placement, and a specific staff member may be an excellent resource if they are familiar with engineering graduate study.

- Many graduate programs and departments will have staff members in roles to help recruit students and assist in the admissions process. Some individuals will assist in a very broad sense with graduate engineering admissions, while others will be quite focused on their particular program or department. Those who help in a very broad sense with your best interests at heart can be invaluable to the prospective student and applicant.

- Especially since the COVID pandemic, there are more opportunities to learn about programs through online information sessions offered by universities or through organizations such as Tau Beta Pi and GEM.

Graduate school admission can be an exciting time but also a very stressful time. Planning early and relying on others to assist you can help immensely and lower the stress level. Reach out to others for invaluable assistance.

Getting the Word Out about Graduate Engineering Opportunities

High school counselors

Many high school counselors help students and parents focus on securing undergraduate admissions at the best colleges and universities. It is not that difficult to identify outstanding high school students who will be prime candidates for graduate study after completing an undergraduate degree. Looking ahead with students and their parents can help introduce them to the opportunities and benefits of a graduate degree, especially in engineering. Much of the work of high school counselors is to help introduce students to the myriad of opportunities that lie ahead. Graduate school can be one of those opportunities.

Higher education advisors, faculty, and career counselors

Once again there is an opportunity for key people in higher education to help educate undergraduate students about graduate study and the benefits of having a graduate degree. This can be accomplished as early as the freshman year in college. It is the experience of the author that most university staff and faculty in engineering schools focus on helping students complete their degrees and find employment opportunities after the completion of an undergraduate degree in engineering. It is not that hard to identify outstanding undergraduate students and help educate them about graduate studies in engineering.

Parents

Parents of strong high school and college students can educate themselves about summer programs, research opportunities, and the long-term benefits of having a graduate degree in engineering, especially immediately following the completion of the undergraduate degree. Parents should be supportive of their sons and daughters as they contemplate their options after the completion of an undergraduate degree. Graduate degrees are lifetime investments that can lead to a better and more fulfilling career.

Employers

Many undergraduate engineering students complete summer internships or even summer research programs at universities. It is important for employers to help identify outstanding talent and encourage them to be open to many options, including graduate school in engineering. This is a clear way for employers to help develop a pipeline of talent with advanced degrees.

Many top engineering students are enrolled in B.S./M.S. programs, which gives them an opportunity to leave the undergraduate university with two degrees. Instead of employing a student with only a bachelor's degree, the employer can delay hiring the graduate until they have completed the master's degree. Some companies are already doing this by holding out the offer until the master's degree is completed.

Final Thoughts

First, congratulations on reaching this point in the book. It is hoped that this guidance will pay great dividends as you contemplate engineering graduate study and hopefully apply for graduate admission.

- Completing graduate study in engineering is a great investment in your future career.
- Most students apply at the end of undergraduate study when they are best prepared to undertake graduate study.
- You can never have too much education.
- Be well-prepared and patient in all that you do.
- Read websites and educate yourself with every application you submit. While there are similarities with your applications, each university and program can be quite different.
- This takes considerable time and research to submit strong applications.
- Turn to others when you need help along the journey.
- Much of what you will experience in graduate study is going to be a marathon and then a sprint in the end.
- On a limited basis and at the discretion of the author, he is willing to respond to questions and feedback. He can be reached at brucealindvall@outlook.com.

Best wishes to each of you in the graduate engineering admissions process!

(Signature)

Resources

American Society for Engineering Education

Big Ten Academic Alliance

Council of Graduate Schools

GEM

National Science Foundation

www.ingramcontent.com/pod-product-compliance
Lightning Source LLC
Chambersburg PA
CBHW041153110526
44590CB00027B/4216